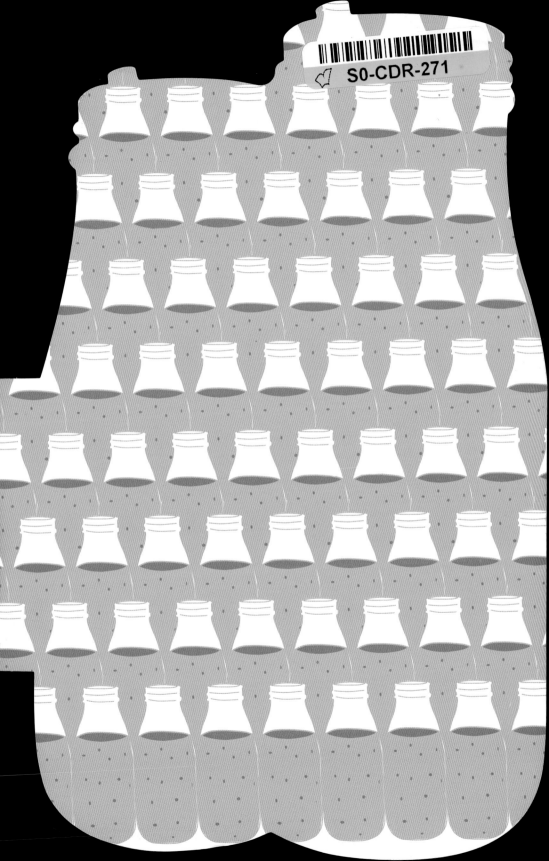

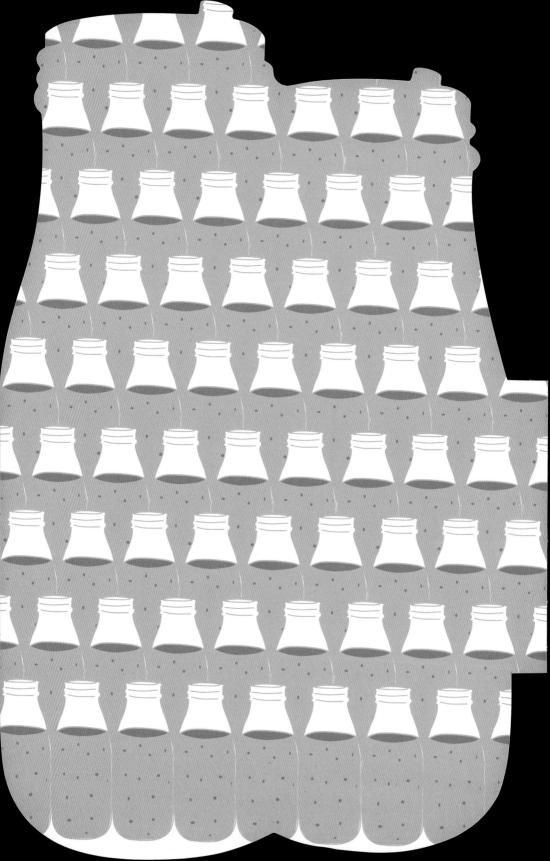

# JUICES AND SMOOTHIES

## 50 Easy Recipes

PHOTOGRAPHS AND RECIPES
CINZIA TRENCHI

GRAPHIC LAYOUT
VALENTINA GIAMMARINARO

# TABLE OF CONTENTS

# JUICES AND SMOOTHIES

Juices and smoothies are a viable and healthy option for breakfast or as an energy snack, quick to make and great allies for any type of diet, as well as beneficial for maintaining your well-being.

These recipes offer myriad possibilities for adding color and flavor to any meal: it takes just a few minutes to fill a glass with something tasty, thanks to the creamy textures of smoothies or the smooth liquid textures of juices.

With little effort we can recharge ourselves with minerals and vitamins, as long as we use ripe fruit and seasonal foods!

It becomes really easy to follow the World Health Organization's recommendations on a healthy diet, based on five portions of fruit and vegetables a day. Each month of the year we can choose which foods to complement our diet with, which is often characterized by ready meals, eaten in a hurry, high in sugar, fat and protein. Fruits and vegetables are complete foods that nature offers us, providing different compounds to help us overcome the cold, heat and discomfort caused by climate change, depending on the seasons. It also appears that the rich variety of colors in the world of fruits and vegetables acts positively on our health: the yellow of lemons, peaches and peppers promises flavonoids and vitamin C; the red of cherries, strawberries and tomatoes emphasizes the presence of lycopene and anthocyanins; the blue of blueberries, plums and grapes suggests a bundle of vitamin C, beta-carotene, potassium and magnesium; finally, the white of fennel, onions, apples and pears indicates the presence of polyphenols, flavonoids, vitamin C and folic acid.

Colors definitely cheer us up, as well as whetting our appetite, and when combined with the inviting fragrance of fruits, vegetables, herbs and spices, they are a resource for both adults and kids! Although it is natural to associate smoothies and juices with hot summer days, their ability to quench our thirst, hydrate and re-mineralize means that they are beneficial year-round: after practicing sports or during a long day in

front of the computer, pepping you up without leaving a heavy feeling in your stomach thanks to the balance of the substances they contain. There is no such thing as a smoothie that doesn't leave you feeling satiated without feeling full. So what are the rules for making appetizing, light and healthy snacks? Always use fresh fruits that smell good, seasonal and preferably organic so that we can also use the peel, for example in the case of apples, pears and peaches.

It is preferable to scrub rather than peel root vegetables like carrots; if hygiene is indispensable, you can use a teaspoon of baking soda to wash fruits and vegetables. Personal taste is the deciding factor when choosing whether to make a juice or a smoothie, as is having the juicer to make the juice; there are many appliances on the market and the latest models are able to get the most from the foods used. However, this system eliminates almost all fibers present in the ingredients and reduces the benefits of the food's intrinsic properties; for this reason it is best to alternate juices with smoothies, or use them to dilute the latter. A smoothie, on the other hand, retains all the nutrients and is great for breakfast or as a snack at any time of the day.

### Sweet and savory smoothies; which milk?

A smoothie is perfect when combined with a little milk; it increases the creaminess and makes it velvety, ideal for a hearty snack, especially for kids or those with little appetite. However, in our recipes we have replaced cow's milk with vegetable substitutes, such as soy, rice, coconut, oat and almond milks; viable alternatives to those derived from animals in terms of flavor and texture. For savory versions, soy milk or soy yogurt are versatile allies that can transform a smoothie into a creamy and flavorsome soup that can replace a first course. Rice milk is also a worthy alternative to cow's milk; with its sweet-neutral taste, it can be used for both savory and sweet smoothies and is also available unsweetened (without added sugar), emphasizing the natural sweetness of the fruits and other ingredients.

Thanks to its high fat, protein and sugar content, oat milk produces smooth and creamy smoothies, perfect for a more substantial snack, helping to maintain concentration and energy, thereby providing valuable assistance to students while studying and sportspeople during physical exertion. You should always have almond milk to hand, and instead of buying it, you can easily make it at home. Shell about 1 1/2 cups (250 g) of almonds; immerse them in boiling water and, once drained, chop them finely. Leave the paste to infuse in a liter of water overnight, and then pass the mixture through a sieve until the milk is white and dense. You can also find almond flour in stores, in which case you can just skip straight to the infusion.

Besides being delicious, coconut milk is a source of energy and perfect for sweetening any smoothie. This too can be homemade: take a whole coconut and mix the liquid inside with the finely grated pulp.

## Ally foods

Each fruit and each vegetable has its own unique characteristics, elements that nature generously offers for our survival and health; each of which, in its entirety, is a small brick that contributes to constructing our well-being. Each has its own distinctive flavor: some are wonderful, others neutral, a few leave us indifferent, but they are all allies; you just need to choose and use them according to their ripeness. Eating an out-of-season strawberry is risky, if you are lucky it will taste like water but it is more likely to be sour, as are apricots and peaches; or in the case of unripe grapes, mouth-puckering and woody, and so on. Vice versa, if you use them when they are ripe, they offer us extremely satisfying aromas and flavors. The texture and color of a ripe fruit are also intense, blueberries for example, which in summer are the color of blue ink and when bitten seem to blend into your taste buds; or fully ripe cherries with intensely red pulp which is

pleasantly a little firm to the bite. Or lettuces, which in spring are tinged with bright green, and the cool tones of cabbages, rich in vitamin C, and so forth.

And tropical fruits? They are always present in supermarkets and therefore available year-round; it's easy to be seduced by pineapples, mangoes, papayas, passion fruit, bananas and avocados. It's worth knowing that pineapple, compact and fragrant with consistent yellow flesh, is great in both juices and smoothies. Banana is a fantastic base ingredient because it sweetens and makes any smoothie velvety and creamy. Mango is risky; often lack of ripeness makes it stringy, but its flavor is still delicious. Papaya is excellent both in juices and smoothies thanks to the high water content of its soft pulp. Avocado plays an important role in our recipes. With its adaptable flavor, this fruit/vegetable can be used with both sweet and savory foods, but its main contribution is its consistency; when blended, it becomes smooth, creamy, soft and compact, making any smoothie uniformly smooth. Thanks to its fat content (also useful for lowering cholesterol), it can be a pleasant and healthy alternative to olive oil for adding flavor to both juices and smoothies!

The "Juices and Smoothies" volume offers fifty very easy and quick-to-prepare recipes, divided into five sections: thirst-quenching juices; re-mineralizing juices and smoothies; energy-boosting juices and smoothies; sweet and savory snacks. Extra virgin olive oil, salt, spices and aromatic herbs are tasty condiments, in addition to being healthy, and ensure that our recipes result in good, appetizing and satisfying creations. The book is designed to inspire you, to help you find your favorite combinations; it suggests sweet combinations that don't require the addition of sugar and sweeteners, with a few exceptions, thanks to the intrinsic characteristics of fruits that, upon fully ripening, contain the right proportion of natural sugars to make them delicious. And for when it is really hot, frozen fruits can be used to make smoothies that resemble sorbets in their texture and freshness.

# THIRST-QUENCHING

# PINEAPPLE, BANANA AND PAPAYA JUICE

### INGREDIENTS FOR **2** SERVINGS

10 1/2 oz. (300 g) pineapple
7 oz. (200 g) papaya
1 banana

### PREPARATION

Remove the skin of the pineapple and cut the fruit into small pieces.
Peel the papaya, remove the seeds and cut into pieces.
Pass the fruit through the centrifugal juicer and collect the juice.
Peel and slice the banana and blend together with the papaya
and pineapple juice. Pour into a pitcher and, if you like, add ice.
This drink refreshes and rehydrates, but it also leaves you feeling
pleasantly satiated; perfect for a light and satisfying snack.

Preparation time: 10' - Difficulty: easy

# CHERRY JUICE SMOOTHIE WITH FROZEN FOREST FRUIT

### INGREDIENTS FOR **2** SERVINGS

1 1/2 cups (300 g) cherries
10 strawberries
10 raspberries
5 blackberries

### PREPARATION

In addition to not having to add ice, frozen fruit make drinks pleasantly dense. The addition of juice, in this case cherry, creates a balanced smoothie that is full of natural sugars, providing a healthy alternative to a packaged snack.
To freeze the fruit: wash and drain the forest fruits, put them on a plate and leave them in the freezer for about 2 hours.
When you are ready to prepare the drink, wash the cherries, leaving a few aside, remove the pit and put them in the centrifugal juicer. Collect the juice and pour it into the blender; add the frozen fruit and blend until the mixture is smooth.
Divide the drink between the glasses, add the remaining cherries and serve.

Preparation time: 5' - Resting time: 2h
Difficulty: easy

# RASPBERRY
# AND BLUEBERRY JUICE

**INGREDIENTS FOR 2 SERVINGS**

2 cups (300 g) raspberries
2/3 cup (100 g) blueberries
4 tbsp. orange juice
2 tbsp. lemon juice

### PREPARATION

Clean the forest fruits carefully and remove any unhealthy berries that could affect the taste of the juice.
Wash the forest fruits separately: put the raspberries in a small colander and rinse them under a slow stream of water; leave the blueberries to soak in water for a few minutes.
Drain the raspberries and blueberries, pass them through the centrifugal juicer and, if you want a really cold juice, blend in the blender with five ice cubes until they are completely crushed.
Pour the smoothie into the glasses and serve immediately.
This is a very healthy drink due to the vitamin C, beta-carotene and folic acid present in the forest fruits.

Preparation time: 10' - Difficulty: easy

# TANGERINE, LEMON AND KIWI JUICE

**INGREDIENTS FOR 2 SERVINGS**

6 tangerines
1 lemon
4 kiwis

PREPARATION

Cut the tangerines and lemon in half and squeeze them; pour
the juice into the blender.
Peel the kiwis, cut into small pieces and add to the citrus fruit juice.
If you want to increase the thirst-quenching power of the drink,
add five ice cubes.
Blend until soft and creamy, then pour into the glasses
and serve immediately.
An excellent source of vitamin C with a great taste: these are
the nutritional characteristics of this drink, which in addition to being
thirst-quenching, can help with rehydration in autumn and winter,
when feeling a little thirsty after passing time in a heated room.

Preparation time: 5' - Difficulty: easy

# MELON JUICE WITH RASPBERRIES, BLACKBERRIES AND BLUEBERRIES

### INGREDIENTS FOR **2** SERVINGS

1 Cantaloupe melon
1 lemon
2/3 cup (100 g) raspberries
3 tbsp. (20 g) blueberries
3 tbsp. (20 g) blackberries

### PREPARATION

Wash the forest fruits, set aside 1/5 for decoration and put the rest in the freezer. This way the juice will already be very cold, rich in nutrients, without adding ice or having to put it in the refrigerator, which would alter its nutritional value.
Squeeze the lemon; peel the melon, remove the seeds, cut into small pieces and pass through the centrifugal juicer.
Pour the lemon and melon juices into the blender and add the frozen forest fruits. Blend for a few seconds until the mixture is ice-cold, creamy and velvety.
Pour into the glasses, decorate with the fruit you set aside and serve immediately.

Preparation time: 5' - Difficulty: easy

# PEAR, FENNEL AND DAIKON JUICE

### INGREDIENTS FOR **2** SERVINGS

7 oz. (200 g) daikon
2 pears
1 fennel
1 tbsp. extra virgin olive oil
salt and pepper
1 small tsp. cress seeds

### PREPARATION

Wash the pears, fennel and daikon, then peel the pears, remove
the core and cut into small pieces. Peel or scrub the daikon
and also cut into pieces.
Clean the fennel, cut into four pieces and leave to soak so as to remove
any soil residue. Leave for 5 minutes, then rinse and drain.
Put 1/4 of the fennel and half of the pears into the blender.
Blend until the puree is uniformly smooth.
Pass the pears, daikon and fennel through the centrifugal juicer,
then stir the juice into the smoothie; season with oil, salt and pepper
and pour into the glasses.
Sprinkle with cress seeds and serve.
Refreshing, cooling and appetizing, this makes a fantastic snack,
especially for those who also love savory flavors in juices.

Preparation time: 15' - Difficulty: easy

# TOMATO, SPRING ONION AND LEMONGRASS JUICE

INGREDIENTS FOR **2** SERVINGS

10 cherry tomatoes
2 spring onions
1 lemon
5 ice cubes
1 sprig of lemongrass
salt and pepper

PREPARATION

Wash and cut the tomatoes in half or into pieces and pass six through
the centrifugal juicer. Put the juice to one side.
Wash the spring onions, put a few green parts to one side
for decoration and pass the rest through the centrifugal juicer;
add the juice to that obtained from the tomatoes.
Wash the lemongrass, divide it into three pieces and put the part
nearest the root (which is softer and more aromatic) in the blender
together with the remaining tomatoes and the ice. Blend until creamy
and uniformly smooth.
Mix the juice and the smoothie together, salt and pepper to taste
and divide equally between the glasses.
Decorate with the remaining pieces of lemongrass and spring onion
and serve immediately.
A thirst-quenching drink, full of flavor, fresh and full of summertime
scents; a favorite for those who prefer to rehydrate their bodies
with tasty savory juices.

Preparation time: 5' - Difficulty: easy

# CELERY, APPLE AND LEMON JUICE

### INGREDIENTS FOR **2** SERVINGS

1lb. (500 g) organic green celery
2 organic apples
1 lemon
salt and pepper (optional)

### PREPARATION

This juice is extremely thirst-quenching and refreshing, the perfect mix for a cooling aperitif, delicious either as it is or seasoned with salt and pepper to taste.
Wash the apples and lemon; soak the celery in water with a tablespoon of baking soda; drain, cut into small pieces and pass through the centrifugal juicer.
Remove the core and seeds from the apples, cut into small pieces without removing the skin and pass through the centrifugal juicer.
Squeeze the lemon, filter the juice and stir it into the celery and apple juice; divide equally between the glasses.
Serve at room temperature, as it is or seasoned with salt and pepper, or with ice.

Preparation time: 15' - Difficulty: easy

# GRAPE AND CUCUMBER JUICE SCENTED WITH LEMON, MINT AND CILANTRO

### INGREDIENTS FOR **2** SERVINGS

1 1/2 cups (200 g) grapes
2 cucumbers
2 radishes
1 lemon
2 sprigs of cilantro
2 sprigs of mint
salt (optional)

### PREPARATION

Wash the grapes, cucumbers and radishes. Take the grapes off
the stems, remove the skin of the cucumbers and the radish leaves.
Cut the vegetables into small pieces and pass all of the ingredients
through the centrifugal juicer at the same time. Squeeze the lemon
and stir the juice into the grape and vegetable juice.
Add a pinch of salt and divide equally between the glasses, scent
with a sprig of cilantro and mint and serve.
This juice is extremely refreshing and has a pronounced flavor;
it is also great served with a few ice cubes or diluted with cold water.
It is low in calories and ideal on hot summer days or after exercise.

Preparation time: 10' - Difficulty: easy

# GREEN TEA WITH DATES AND LETTUCE

INGREDIENTS FOR **2** SERVINGS

2 1/2 cups (100 g) lettuce leaves
2 bananas
2 pitted dates
1 tsp. green tea leaves

PREPARATION

Bring 1 1/2 cups (3 dl) of water to the boil; switch off, add the tea leaves and leave to infuse.
After five minutes filter the tea and leave to cool.
Clean and wash the lettuce, tear into bits and put in the blender.
Peel and slice the banana and put it in the blender; add the dates and green tea and turn on.
It takes just a few seconds to prepare this tasty refreshing drink, rich in antioxidants and suitable for both adults and kids.

Preparation time: 10' - Cooling time: 20'
Difficulty: easy

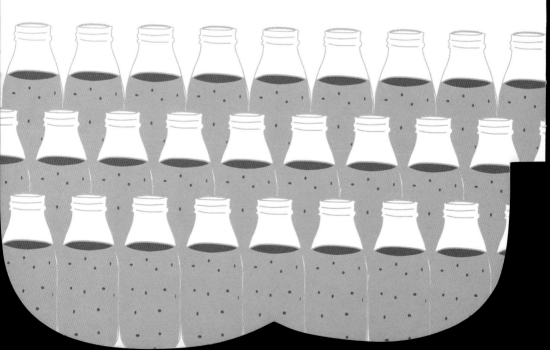

32

# RE-MINERALIZING

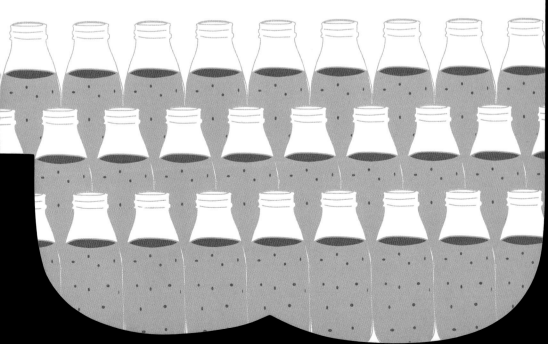

# COCOA SMOOTHIE

INGREDIENTS FOR **2** SERVINGS

1 cup (2 dl) almond milk
2 plums
1 peach
1 tbsp. unsweetened cocoa powder (about 10 g)
2 tsp. cane sugar (about 10 g)

PREPARATION

Wash the plums and the peach, remove the pits, cut into small pieces
and put in the blender. Add the sugar, cocoa powder and almond milk.
Blend for a few seconds until the smoothie is smooth,
creamy and thick.
Pour into the glasses and serve immediately.
This nutritious smoothie is tasty, appetizing, popular with children
at breakfast or as a snack, and very quick to prepare.
However, it is not recommended in the evening, as the theobromine
present in the cocoa powder is a stimulant and can disrupt sleep,
especially in children.

Preparation time: 5' - Difficulty: easy

# ALMOND MILK SMOOTHIE WITH POMEGRANATE AND PEAR JUICE

### INGREDIENTS FOR **2** SERVINGS

2 cups (4 dl) almond milk
2 pears
1/4 cup (50 g) pomegranate juice

### PREPARATION

Wash and peel the pears, remove the seeds and core, cut into small
pieces and put in the blender. Add the pomegranate juice
and almond milk.
Blend until very smooth and pink, which can range from pale
to a stronger much shade, depending on the amount of pomegranate
juice and the color of the seeds used.
A wonderful drink to quell your hunger, deliciously light and tasty;
besides tasting good, it is thirst-quenching, energy boosting and great
for recharging without feeling full.

Preparation time: 10' - Difficulty: easy

# RICE MILK, ORANGE AND APPLE SMOOTHIE

**INGREDIENTS FOR 2 SERVINGS**

2 cups (4 dl) rice milk
1 organic red apple
1 orange

PREPARATION

Squeeze the orange, filter the juice and pour into the blender.
Wash the apple, leaving about half the peel, remove the core
and seeds and cut into small pieces.
Add it to the orange juice together with the rice milk and blend
until the mixture is uniformly smooth.
Pour into a bottle and drink it throughout the morning to restore
your strength, at the same time helping you not to snack
in order to curb your hunger.

Preparation time: 10' - Difficulty: easy

# APRICOT AND MEDLAR SMOOTHIE

**INGREDIENTS FOR 2 SERVINGS**

1lb. (500 g) very ripe medlars
10 ripe apricots

PREPARATION

Wash and peel the medlars, remove the pits and pass the flesh through the centrifugal juicer.
Collect the juice and pour into the blender.
Wash the apricots, remove the pit and add to the medlar juice; blend and divide between the glasses.
Apricots are rich in retinol, vitamins C, B1, B2, PP and minerals: potassium, phosphorus, magnesium, iron and calcium.
To make this smoothie really nice, we recommend you use only ripe medlars because the unripe fruits are astringent and the tannin flavor becomes predominant. Ripe medlars, on the other hand, give the drink a sweet flavor and they are rich in beta carotene, a precursor of vitamin A, very useful in promoting regular bowel function.

Preparation time: 15' - Difficulty: easy

# OAT AND BANANA SMOOTHIE

**INGREDIENTS FOR 2 SERVINGS**

2 cups (4 dl) oat milk
2 small bananas
2 tbsp. oat flakes
1 tbsp. malt

### PREPARATION

Besides being perfect for an energetic breakfast, this smoothie is indicated for those practicing sports or students who have to study and concentrate for long periods of time.
Characterized by its great taste, it only takes a few minutes to make, and if you want to accentuate the natural sweetness of the banana and oat, add the malt.
Peel and slice the bananas and put them in the blender; add the oat flakes and malt and blend for a few seconds, until you get a thick, velvety and very tasty smoothie.

Preparation time: 10' - Difficulty: easy

# AVOCADO AND COCONUT MILK SMOOTHIE

### INGREDIENTS FOR **2** SERVINGS

7 oz. (200 g) avocado (about half of the fruit)
(50 g) fresh coconut
1 cup (2 dl) coconut milk

### PREPARATION

Remove the shell and dark parts of the coconut; cut into small pieces,
leaving a small amount for decoration, then put it in the blender
and add the coconut milk.
Peel the avocado, remove the pit, cut into small pieces and add
to the ingredients in the blender.
Blend until creamy, smooth, thick and soft. Pour into the glasses
and decorate with a piece of coconut.
This drink has a wonderful consistency and is perfect as a light meal
replacement. It is very nutritious and tastes delicious.

Preparation time: 10' - Difficulty: easy

# AVOCADO, GREEN CABBAGE AND CHILI PEPPER SMOOTHIE

### INGREDIENTS FOR **2** SERVINGS

7 oz. (200 g) green cabbage
1 avocado
1 lemon
1 fresh chili pepper, as hot as you like
1/2 cup (1 dl) soy milk
salt and pepper

### PREPARATION

Wash the green cabbage and pass it through the centrifugal juicer.
Squeeze the lemon and filter the juice.
Peel the avocado, remove the pit and cut into small pieces;
put it in the blender.
Wash the chili pepper, cut it into four pieces and remove the seeds.
Put the milk, green cabbage juice and lemon juice in the blender and
add a pinch of salt and pepper to taste. Blend until creamy, then pour
into the glasses and season with the chili pepper.
This creamy, appetizing drink is perfect for a healthy break thanks
to the high concentration of vitamin C present in the green cabbage,
chili pepper and lemon.

Preparation time: 10' - Difficulty: easy

# BEET AND CITRUS FRUIT SMOOTHIE

INGREDIENTS FOR **2** SERVINGS

14 oz. (400 g) roasted red beet
1 lemon
1 tangerine
salt and pepper
a few beet leaves for decoration
a few edible flowers for decoration
4 slices of organic lemon for decoration
1 tbsp. extra virgin olive oil (optional)
1 tbsp. vinegar (optional)

PREPARATION

This smoothie is an excellent light meal replacement.
It is thirst-quenching and energy-boosting, indicated for sportspeople
and those who need to concentrate for a long period of time.
The citrus fruit balance the slightly earthy and sweet taste of the beet
and adding seasoning can make it an even more appetizing drink.
Peel the beets, cut into small pieces and pass half of the amount
through the centrifugal juicer.
Pour the juice into the blender, add the remaining beets
and the freshly squeezed and filtered citrus fruit juice.
Blend until creamy and uniformly smooth, then divide equally
between the glasses.
Season to taste, decorate with the leaves, lemon slices, edible flowers
and serve.

Preparation time: 10' - Difficulty: easy

# TOMATO, PEPPER, CHILI PEPPER AND BROCCOLI SMOOTHIE

### INGREDIENTS FOR **2** SERVINGS

7 oz. (200 g) broccoli
4 tomatoes
1/2 yellow pepper
1 fresh medium hot chili pepper
2 tbsp. extra virgin olive oil
1 tbsp. apple vinegar
salt

### PREPARATION

Wash and peel the tomatoes, remove the seeds and cut into small pieces; put into the blender. Clean the pepper, remove the seeds and white parts and cut into small pieces; add to the tomatoes. Wash the chili pepper, remove the stalk and seeds and cut into small pieces; add to the other ingredients together with the oil, salt to taste and vinegar.
Blend until uniformly smooth, pour into the glasses and serve with the remaining thinly sliced broccoli.

Preparation time: 15' - Difficulty: easy

# ALMOND FROZEN YOGURT SMOOTHIE WITH RAISINS

### INGREDIENTS FOR **2** SERVINGS

1 1/2 cups (300 g) almond milk frozen yogurt
3 tbsp. (20 g) raisins
3 tbsp. (20 g) blanched almonds
1 cup (2 dl) almond milk
2 tbsp. Rum (optional)

### PREPARATION

Naturally sweet thanks to the almonds, which give it a delicious flavor, this smoothie makes a perfect snack for a healthy but very enjoyable break! Make it just before you serve it so as to fully enjoy the flavors and nutritional benefits, although this drink does not lose its properties and flavor if kept in the refrigerator for a day or two.
Put the frozen yogurt, milk, raisins and almonds in the blender; blend at maximum speed until all the ingredients are well mixed, then pour into the glasses.
You can also serve it as a dessert; add a little Rum to make it perfect.

Preparation time: 10' - Difficulty: easy

# ENERGY BOOSTING

# DATE, RAISIN AND COCOA SMOOTHIE WITH WHEAT FLAKES AND ALMOND MILK

### INGREDIENTS FOR **2** SERVINGS

1 cup (2 dl) almond milk
1/2 cup (50 g) pitted dates
1/2 cup (40 g) wheat flakes
1/4 cup (20 g) raisins
1 tbsp. (about 10 g) unsweetened cocoa powder

### PREPARATION

Soak the raisins and dates in lukewarm milk for 10 minutes.
Put the milk mixture and dry fruit in the blender, add the cocoa powder
and half of the wheat flakes. Blend until uniformly smooth.
Divide between the glasses or bowls and serve with the remaining
wheat flakes.
This smoothie makes a great breakfast for students and sportspeople.
Light, nutritious and satisfying, there is no need to add sugar thanks
to the sweetening power of the dates and raisins. It is also a natural
stimulant thanks to the cocoa, helping you to stay concentrated
and feel full of energy.

Preparation time: 20' - Difficulty: easy

# COCONUT MILK SMOOTHIE WITH PISTACHIO NUTS

**INGREDIENTS FOR 2 SERVINGS**

1/2 cup (100 g) coconut sorbet
1/4 cup (20 g) plain Bronte pistachio nuts
1 cup (2 dl) coconut milk

PREPARATION

This simple smoothie is delicious thanks to the freshness of the sorbet, which makes it just as tasty as an ice cream, but without having to feel guilty about too many calories, sugar and added fats.
Coconut is rich in fats beneficial to your health and is accompanied by the deliciously tantalizing flavor of the pistachios.
Put all of the ingredients in the blender (setting aside half of the pistachio nuts) and blend until uniformly smooth.
Pour into the glasses, sprinkle with the remaining pistachio nuts and serve.

Preparation time: 5' - Difficulty: easy

# ALMOND MILK SMOOTHIE WITH DRY FRUIT AND GOJI BERRIES

### INGREDIENTS FOR **2** SERVINGS

1/4 cup (20 g) Goji berries
1 cup (2 dl) almond milk
4 dried figs
10 blanched almonds

### PREPARATION

Heat half the milk gently until it reaches 40 degrees; add the Goji
berries and dried figs, without the pit and cut into small pieces,
and leave to soak for 10 minutes.
Put in the fridge and leave to cool.
Put the milk, the drained Goji berries and figs and almonds
in the blender and blend until the liquid becomes uniformly smooth.
Pour into the glasses and serve.
Great as a snack or for breakfast, this is an energy boosting drink full
of vitamins and minerals. It is perfect at room temperature, but if you
want a more refreshing smoothie add five or six ice cubes.

Preparation time: 20' - Difficulty: easy

# ALMOND MILK SMOOTHIE WITH GRAPES AND FOREST FRUITS

**INGREDIENTS FOR 2 SERVINGS**

1/2 cup (1 dl) almond milk
2 1/2 cups (100 g) raspberries
1/3 cup (30 g) blackberries
1/3 cup (30 g) blueberries
10 grapes
1/4 cup (0,5 dl) raspberry juice

**For the skewers:**
10 blackberries
2 grapes
8 blueberries
4 raspberries

### PREPARATION

Wash the fruit separately, drain them and put the best ones to one side for the skewers.

Put the raspberries, blackberries, blueberries, grapes and raspberry juice in the blender; blend until uniformly smooth.

If you prefer a mixture without seeds, pass the fruit through a sieve before putting them in the blender.

Finally, add the almond milk and blend again for a few seconds to ensure that it is well-mixed.

Prepare the skewers with the fruit that you put aside, being as creative as you like.

Divide between the glasses, decorate with the fruit skewers and serve.

A wonderfully delicious drink, cool, refreshing and full of useful substances beneficial to your wellbeing, such as vitamins in the forest fruits, minerals in the grapes and antioxidants in the almond milk.

Preparation time: 10' - Difficulty: easy

# PEACH AND MELON SMOOTHIE

### INGREDIENTS FOR **2** SERVINGS

1 1/2 cups (300 g) melon sorbet
7 oz. (200 g) Cantaloupe melon
4 organic yellow peaches
5 ice cubes

### PREPARATION

Wash the peaches, remove the pit, cut into small pieces and put in the blender. Remove the skin from the melon, scoop out the seeds, cut into small pieces and add to the peaches.
Add the sorbet and ice and blend until the smoothie is thick, creamy, refreshing and thirst-quenching.
Perfect on hot days, the wealth of vitamins and minerals present in the fruits, as well as it being low calorie, make this smoothie great for satisfying your hunger without feeling full.

Preparation time: 5' - Difficulty: easy

# CHERRY SYRUP WITH VANILLA SOY ICE CREAM

INGREDIENTS FOR **2** SERVINGS
2 1/2 lb. (1 kg) cherries
2 cups (400 g) soy ice cream
1/2 cup (100 g) cane sugar

PREPARATION

Wash the cherries, remove the stalks and pits, and put about ten
of them aside; cook over a medium flame together with the cane sugar,
stirring regularly so as avoid the mixture sticking to the bottom
of the pan.
Leave to cook for about 30 minutes, then remove from the heat
and leave to cool. Roughly chop the remaining cherries, mix into the ice
cream and put back into the freezer for 20 minutes.
When you are ready to serve, divide the ice cream between two bowls
and cover it with about 1/2 cup (1 dl) of cherry syrup.
Leave the two ingredients to absorb for about 3-4 minutes, then serve.
If you like, you can add some cherries in syrup and keep the rest
in a closed jar in the refrigerator for a few days.
This drink is very tasty, nutritious, perfect for children and those
with no appetite, and ideal on hot summer days.
To prepare the cherries in syrup, you can also use fruit that is not
particularly good to look at or too ripe to be served at the table

Preparation time: 20' - Cooling time: 20 minutes
Cooking time: 30 minutes - Difficulty: easy

# ORANGE JUICE, APPLE AND MALT SMOOTHIE

**INGREDIENTS FOR 2 SERVINGS**

2 apples
2 oranges
2 tbsp. malt (about 20 g)

### PREPARATION

Squeeze the oranges and pour the juice into the blender.
Wash and peel the apples, remove the core, cut into small pieces and
add to the orange juice. Add the malt and blend until velvety
and uniformly smooth.
Pour into the glasses and serve.
Ideal for breakfast or a nutrient-rich snack, this smoothie is particularly
suitable for children or people who need an energy boost, but who
don't have time to stop playing or working! Really quick to make,
this drink is a source of energy year-round; for a more refreshing
version in summer, just add five or six ice cubes while making.

Preparation time: 5' - Difficulty: easy

# APPLE JUICE
# WITH GRAPEFRUIT, LEMON
# AND TANGERINE

### INGREDIENTS FOR **2** SERVINGS

2 pink grapefruits
2 organic apples
2 organic lemons
2 tangerines

### PREPARATION

Wash the apples, remove the core and seeds, cut into small pieces
and pass them through the centrifugal juicer; pour the juice
into a pitcher.
Cut the grapefruits and tangerines in half; squeeze and add
to the apple juice.
Wash the lemons; squeeze one and slice the other. Add the juice
and lemon slices to the pitcher, stir and serve.
This drink combines the tartness of the lemon with the grapefruit's
slight bitterness, and the sweetness of the tangerine with the freshness
of the apple. It is an excellent thirst-quenching blend, perfect on hot
days after a hard work-out.

Preparation time: 10' - Difficulty: easy

# PEACH JUICE WITH RASPBERRIES, BLACKBERRIES AND BLUEBERRIES

### INGREDIENTS FOR **2** SERVINGS

2 ripe peaches
2/3 cup (100 g) blueberries
2/3 cup (100 g) blackberries
2/3 cup (100 g) raspberries

### PREPARATION

Wash the forest fruits and put them in the freezer to freeze.
When you are ready to make the juice, wash the peaches, remove the pit, cut into small pieces and pass them through the centrifugal juicer; pour the juice into the blender.
Add the frozen forest fruits and blend until uniformly smooth.
The result will be a thick, cold, thirst-quenching and energy boosting drink, perfect on hot summer days. It is also ideal as a rehydration drink, and if you want it to be colder you can add as many ice cubes as you like.

Preparation time: 5' - Cooling time: 1 h 40'
Difficulty: easy

# GRAPEFRUIT JUICE WITH PAPAYA, STRAWBERRIES AND PLUMS

### INGREDIENTS FOR **2** SERVINGS

3 1/2 oz. (100 g) ripe papaya
3 1/2 oz. (100 g) avocado
1 pink grapefruit
1 banana
5 strawberries
2 plums
4 winter cherries

### PREPARATION

Squeeze the grapefruit and filter the juice; put it in the blender.
Wash the strawberries and plums, cut into small pieces, remove
the pit from the plums and the stalk from the strawberries; add
to the grapefruit juice. Remove the skin and seeds from the papaya
and mango, cut both into small pieces and add to the other ingredients.
Peel the banana and put in the blender.
Blend until uniformly smooth, distribute equally between the glasses
and decorate with the winter cherries.
This smoothie is a triumph of colors and flavors combined with a rich
and appetizing mixture of fruit. Thirst quenching and nutritious,
it is a tasty snack that is full of energy.

Preparation time: 20' - Difficulty: easy

# SWEET SNACKS

# PINEAPPLE, MANGO, PAPAYA AND PASSION FRUIT SMOOTHIE

### INGREDIENTS FOR **2** SERVINGS

7 oz. (200 g) pineapple
7 oz. (200 g) papaya
1 cup (2 dl) melon juice
1 mango
4 passion fruits

### PREPARATION

Remove the skin from the pineapple, cut into pieces and put
in the blender. Peel the mango, remove the pit, cut into small pieces
and add to the pineapple.
Clean the papaya, remove the skin and seeds, cut into small pieces
and add to the other ingredients. Add the melon juice and blend until
uniformly smooth, runny and well-mixed. Pour into the glasses
and serve with the passion fruits cut in half.
A delicious smoothie, full of flavor, color and freshness. Take
a decadent break with a naturally sweet snack, which offers many
benefits in the form of vitamins and minerals, such as vitamin C, retinol,
potassium and last, but not least, with few calories!

Preparation time: 10' - Difficulty: easy

# SMOOTHIE WITH BANANA, CAROB, HAZELNUTS AND SOY MILK

### INGREDIENTS FOR **2** SERVINGS

3 tbsp. (20 g) carob powder
2 tbsp. (20 g) shelled hazelnuts
1 1/2 cups (3 dl) soy milk
2 bananas

### PREPARATION

Roughly chop the hazelnuts and put them in the blender together with the soy milk and peeled and sliced bananas. Add the carob powder and blend until uniformly smooth.
Pour into the glasses and serve at room temperature.
Great for its high content of minerals like potassium, calcium and iron, this smoothie is a healthy, nutritious snack that can also be served with the addition of a teaspoon of cane sugar or malt.
This smoothie is an ideal replacement for chocolate drinks, especially for children.

Preparation time: 5' - Difficulty: easy

# APRICOT SMOOTHIE WITH BLUEBERRIES, BLACKBERRIES AND COCONUT MILK

### INGREDIENTS FOR **2** SERVINGS

10 apricots
1/2 cup (100 g) coconut milk
1/2 cup (50 g) frozen blackberries
1/2 cup (40 g) frozen blueberries

### PREPARATION

Wash and drain all the fruit, then put the berries on a plate and put them in the freezer to chill for about two hours.
When you are ready to make the drink, wash the apricots, remove the pit, cut into small pieces and put in the blender; add the coconut milk and the frozen fruit. Blend until the mixture is uniformly smooth. Divide the drink between the glasses and serve.
This is a wonderful drink, fresh and nutritious, light and easily digestible. It is full of useful elements for guaranteeing your wellbeing: calcium, potassium, phosphorus and vitamins like A, C, E and the B group.

Preparation time: 10' - Resting time: 2 h
Difficulty: easy

# CHERRY, APRICOT
# AND PEACH JUICE SMOOTHIE

### INGREDIENTS FOR **2** SERVINGS

7 oz. (200 g) apricots
1 cup (100 g) cherries
4 very ripe white nectarines
2 apricots and 4 cherries for decoration

### PREPARATION

Wash all the fruit, remove the pits from the cherries and put them
in the blender. Remove the apricot pits, cut the fruit into small pieces
and add to the cherries, leaving a few aside for decoration.
Take three of the nectarines, remove the pits and cut into small pieces;
put in the centrifugal juicer. Collect the juice and pour into the blender.
After removing the pit, cut up the remaining nectarine and add
to the other fruit in the blender. Blend until the mixture is creamy
and uniformly smooth.
With the fruits you set aside, prepare skewers by alternating pieces
of apricot and cherry. Pour the smoothie into the glasses, decorate
with the fruit skewers and serve.
Rich, yummy and thirst-quenching, this makes a delicious snack full
of minerals and vitamins.
In addition to being irresistible, cherries are fruit with antioxidant
and anti-inflammatory properties, and they also have an important
diuretic effect.

Preparation time: 15' - Difficulty: easy

# APPLE, PEAR, GINGER AND LEMON SMOOTHIE WITH SOY YOGURT

### INGREDIENTS FOR **2** SERVINGS

2 pears
1 apple
1 lemon
4 slices of ginger
1 1/2 cups (3 dl) soy yogurt
extra virgin olive oil, salt and pepper (optional)

### PREPARATION

Wash and peel the pears and apples, remove the cores and seeds, cut into small pieces and put them in the blender.
Peel the slices of ginger and add them to the fruit; squeeze the lemon and after having filtered the juice, pour it into the blender.
Add the yogurt and blend until uniformly smooth. Divide equally between the glasses and serve.
This ginger smoothie is a very versatile, slightly sweet drink, excellent as it is, without the need for extra seasoning. However, for those who prefer savory and spicy flavors, just season it with a little oil, salt and pepper for a tasty drink, perfect as an aperitif.

Preparation time: 5' - Difficulty: easy

# WHITE MELON SMOOTHIE WITH SUN-KISSED CHERRIES IN SYRUP

### INGREDIENTS FOR **2** SERVINGS

10 1/2 oz. (300 g) white melon
1/2 cup (100 g) almond milk yogurt

### For the cherries in syrup
2 1/2 lb. (1 kg) ripe cherries
1/2 cup (100 g) cane sugar

### PREPARATION

Prepare the cherries in syrup: wash the cherries, remove the stalk and pit, put into one or more containers; divided the cane sugar equally over the cherries and put the lids on. Leave the containers in direct sunlight for several days, making sure you put them in a safe place overnight.
Within two or three days, the fruit sugars and cane sugar will have dissolved, forming a homogeneous dark syrup. When the lid starts sucking inwards due to the heat, you can put the containers away.
Remove the skin and seeds from the melon, cut into pieces and put in the blender together with the yogurt and half of the cherries, including the syrup.
Blend until uniformly smooth, pour into the glasses and serve together with the remaining cherries in syrup.

Preparation time: 60' - Resting time: 3-4 days
Difficulty: medium

# BLUEBERRY, PLUM AND BANANA SMOOTHIE

### INGREDIENTS FOR **2** SERVINGS
1 1/2 cups (200 g) blueberries
1 cup (2 dl) vanilla rice yogurt
1 cup (2 dl) rice milk
1 banana
4 organic yellow plums

### PREPARATION

Clean, wash and drain the blueberries, patting them lightly to dry them.
Wash the plums, remove the pit, cut into small pieces and put them
in the blender. Add the yogurt, rice milk and blueberries (putting 10
to one side for decoration).
Add the peeled and sliced banana and blend until uniformly smooth.
Divide equally between the glasses, sprinkle with the remaining
blueberries and serve.
You can prepare the smoothie by mixing fresh fruit with ice-cold fruit,
such as frozen blueberries and banana. In this way the drink is
an ice cream replacement, maintaining the characteristics of a healthy,
tasty snack, rich with the valuable benefits of seasonal fruit
and the properties of yogurt.

Preparation time: 10' - Difficulty: easy

# MEDLAR AND PLUM SMOOTHIE

**INGREDIENTS FOR 2 SERVINGS**

14 oz. (400 g) organic apricots
10 1/2 oz. (300 g) medlars
2 organic yellow plums
2 organic red plums
1 banana

**PREPARATION**

Wash and peel the medlars, remove the seeds, cut into small pieces
and put them in the blender. Wash the apricots, remove the pits,
cut into small pieces and pass them through the centrifugal juicer;
pour the juice into the blender.
Wash the plums, remove the pits and cut into small pieces; peel
and slice the banana and add to the blender together with the plums.
Blend until uniformly smooth and then pour into the glasses.
This smoothie is sweet, creamy and nutritious, suitable for kids
and those with not much appetite; there is a concentration of nutrients:
in particular retinol, folic acid and vitamin C.

Preparation time: 10' - Difficulty: easy

# PEAR, MELON, BANANA AND CINNAMON SMOOTHIE

INGREDIENTS FOR **2** SERVINGS

10 1/2 oz. (300 g) white melon
2 pears
1 banana
1/2 cup (1 dl) coconut milk
cinnamon powder
1 tbsp. malt (optional)

PREPARATION

Peel the pears, remove the cores and seeds, cut into small pieces
and put them in the blender.
Clean the melon, remove the skin and seeds and cut into small pieces.
Peel and slice the banana, add it to the melon in the blender together
with the coconut milk.
Add a pinch or 1/2 tsp. of cinnamon (this can vary according to taste)
and blend until uniformly smooth.
Pour into the glasses and serve this delicious, richly flavored smoothie.
Extremely thirst-quenching, it is a satisfying drink to accompany
a break in any season, for both adults and kids.
Harmoniously sweet, it is perfect as it is, but if you prefer something
sweeter, you can add a tsp. of malt or a drop of stevia.

Preparation time: 5' - Difficulty: easy

# MIXED SMOOTHIE
# WITH FROZEN FRUIT

## INGREDIENTS FOR **2** SERVINGS

7 oz. (200 g) mango
7 oz. (200 g) pineapple
2/3cup (100 g) strawberries
1/2 cup (50 g) grapes
1/2 cup (50 g) blueberries
1 banana
1 orange

### PREPARATION

Wash the blueberries, strawberries and grapes. Take the grapes off
the stems and put them in the freezer. The frozen fruit means that you
can make a naturally ice-cold smoothie, without the addition of ice
and with a consistency that is similar to a sorbet.
If you like cold drinks, you can keep a stock of frozen fruit to use
when needed, avoiding fruit that changes color and flavor,
for example: peaches, apricots, oranges and pears.
The following are perfect for freezing: strawberries, blueberries,
blackberries, raspberries and grapes.
Squeeze the orange and pour the juice into the blender; add
the strawberries, the peeled and chopped mango, the pineapple
without the skin and cut into small pieces, and the peeled and sliced
banana. Blend until uniformly smooth and pour into the glasses.
Divide the blueberries between the glasses, stir in and serve.

Preparation time: 10' - Resting time: 1 h 30'
Difficulty: easy

# SAVORY SNACKS

# GAZPACHO

INGREDIENTS FOR **2** SERVINGS

3 cups (400 g) ripe cherry tomatoes
1 cucumber
2 spring onions
1 small white onion
2 tbsp. extra virgin olive oil
1 tbsp. lemon juice
1 tsp. apple vinegar
salt and pepper
2 sprigs of basil

### PREPARATION

Clean the spring onions and basil. Wash, dry and put to one side until you need to use them. Wash the tomatoes and pass them through the centrifugal juicer; put the juice to one side. Peel the onion and cut in half. Wash and peel the cucumber and pass through the centrifugal juicer together with half of the onion. Pour the juices into the blender, add the lemon juice, vinegar, oil, salt and pepper to taste, and the remaining onion; blend until uniformly smooth. Divide equally between the glasses, decorate and scent with the basil and spring onions. If you love cold drinks, you can serve it with ice cubes. Excellent as an aperitif or a snack at any time of the day, this smoothie is thirst-quenching and tasty, characterized by its low calories and strong flavor.

Preparation time: 10' - Difficulty: easy

# AVOCADO SMOOTHIE
# WITH CUCUMBER, SPRING
# ONION AND AROMATIC HERBS

INGREDIENTS FOR **2** SERVINGS

**For the smoothie**
1 very ripe avocado
2 cucumbers
1 lemon
1 spring onion
2 sprigs of anise
2 sprigs of marjoram

2 sprigs of mint
salt

**For the skewers**
1 cucumber
1 spring onion

PREPARATION

Prepare the skewers: wash the spring onion and cucumber.
Peel and slice the cucumber, slice the spring onion and put
the skewers together as you like.
Wash, peel and chop the cucumbers. Clean and slice the spring onion;
pass the cucumbers and half of the spring onion through
the centrifugal juicer. Pour the juice into the blender.
Peel the avocado, remove the pit, cut into pieces and add to
the spring onion and cucumber juice.
Squeeze the lemon, add the juice to the other ingredients, add
the remaining spring onion, half of the aromatic herbs without
the stems, and salt to taste; blend until soft, creamy
and uniformly smooth.
Divide between the glasses, scent and decorate with the remaining
aromatic herbs and serve with the vegetable skewers.

Preparation time: 10' - Difficulty: easy

# CARROT SMOOTHIE
# WITH CABBAGE AND NETTLE

### INGREDIENTS FOR **2** SERVINGS

7 oz. (200 g) Chinese cabbage
2 1/2 cups (100 g) nettles
4 carrots
1 lemon
1 fresh medium hot chili pepper
1 tbsp. extra virgin olive oil
1 sage leaf
salt

### PREPARATION

Wash the chili pepper, remove the stalk and seeds.
Clean the nettles and steam them for 5 minutes; blend them
and then filter the juice. Wash the cabbage, cut into pieces, pass them
through the centrifugal juicer and pour the juice into the blender.
Wash and scrub the carrot, slice into rounds and put them
in the blender. Squeeze the lemon, add the juice to the carrot,
together with salt, chili pepper to taste and the sage;
blend until uniformly smooth.
Serve and enjoy the detoxifying properties of this smoothie,
rich in retinol, folic acid and vitamin C, particularly indicated in spring.

Preparation time: 20' - Cooking time: 5'
Difficulty: easy

# BELGIAN ENDIVE, RADICCHIO AND RADISH SMOOTHIE WITH SOY YOGURT

### INGREDIENTS FOR **2** SERVINGS

1 cup (200 g) soy yogurt
4 radishes
1 head of Belgian endive (about 100 g)
1 head of radicchio (about 150 g)
1 tbsp. extra virgin olive oil
salt and pepper
2 sprigs of fresh rosemary, to decorate and scent

### PREPARATION

Wash the vegetables and cut into small pieces. Pass half
through the centrifugal juicer and pour the juice into the blender.
Add the remaining vegetables, yogurt, salt and pepper to taste and oil.
Blend until thick and smooth. Divide equally between the glasses, scent
with the rosemary and serve.
This makes a great snack, perfect to replace a first course.
This smoothie is rich in vitamins such as folic acid and retinol, fibers
and minerals. The fact that it is low-calorie makes it an ally for feeling
satiated without feeling full.

Preparation time: 15' - Difficulty: easy

# CABBAGE JUICE WITH BROCCOLI, APPLE AND LEMON

**INGREDIENTS FOR 2 SERVINGS**

7 oz. (200 g) Savoy cabbage
7 oz. (200 g) Chinese cabbage
7 oz. (200 g) broccoli
4 green cabbage leaves
1 organic apple
1 lemon
salt

**PREPARATION**

Clean, wash and drain the vegetables; leave them to dry on a tea towel.
Cut into small pieces, putting half of the broccoli to one side, and pass
them through the centrifugal juicer. Pour the juice into a pitcher.
Cut the apple into pieces after having removed the core and seeds,
pass it through the centrifugal juicer and add the juice to
the vegetable juice in the pitcher.
Add the freshly squeezed lemon juice and salt; divide
equally between the glasses.
Serve the drink with the remaining raw broccoli cut into slices.
This drink is a concentration of nutrients such as folic acid, retinol,
vitamin C and minerals such as calcium, potassium and phosphorus.
The apple and lemon soften the strong flavor of the cabbages, making
it a perfect snack for an enjoyable and satisfying break.

Preparation time: 15' - Difficulty: easy

# DAIKON JUICE WITH RADISH, FAVA BEANS AND PEAS

## INGREDIENTS FOR **2** SERVINGS

14 oz. (400 g) daikon
1/2 cup (50 g) shelled peas
1/2 cup (50 g) shelled fava beans
4 radishes
1 green spring onion stalk
1 tbsp. extra virgin olive oil
1 tsp. Umeboshi vinegar
salt and pink pepper

## PREPARATION

Wash and scrub the daikon and cut into small pieces.
Wash the radishes.
Remove the skins from the fava beans and put in a bowl.
Add the peas, 1/5 of the daikon and two sliced radishes.
Pass the remaining daikon and radishes through the centrifugal juicer
and collect the juice. Season with oil, salt, pepper, Umeboshi vinegar
and stir. Add the legumes and divide equally between the glasses.
Great snack or appetizer to serve with sliced vegetables
of your choice. A beneficial juice that should only be made
with the freshest ingredients.

Preparation time: 20' - Difficulty: easy

# PEPPER, ORANGE, CHILI PEPPER AND GINGER JUICE WITH VEGETABLE SKEWERS

INGREDIENTS FOR **2** SERVINGS

**For the juice**
2 oranges
2 tangerines
1 yellow pepper
6 cherry tomatoes
1 lemon
1 chili pepper
1 tsp. grated ginger
salt
2 bunches of cilantro

**For the skewers**
8 cherry tomatoes
8 slices of daikon
4 pieces of yellow pepper
4 slices of ginger
4 organic orange segments with the peel

PREPARATION

Wash the ingredients for the skewers and make four skewers, alternating the different flavors. Put to one side until you are ready to serve the juice. Squeeze the lemon, tangerines and oranges; filter the juice if necessary. Wash the peppers, remove the white parts and seeds, and pass it through the centrifugal juicer. Mix the pepper juice with the citrus fruit juice. Blend the tomatoes and chili pepper and pass them through a sieve; stir in the pepper juice and citrus fruit juice. Add the grated ginger and salt to taste; stir again before dividing the juice equally between the glasses; scent with cilantro and serve with the fruit and vegetable skewers. A great thirst-quencher, full of tantalizing flavors, this juice also makes a tasty appetizer, rich in vitamins and minerals but low in calories.

Preparation time: 15' - Difficulty: easy

# RICE MILK SOUP WITH FRUITS AND VEGETABLES

### INGREDIENTS FOR **2** SERVINGS

1 cup (200 g) rice milk
3 1/2 oz. (100 g) avocado
3 1/2 oz. (100 g) pineapple
3 1/2 oz. (100 g) yellow pepper
2 oz. (50 g) beet
1 Belgian endive (about 100 g)
2 cucumbers

1 spring onion
1 lemon
1 chili pepper
3 sprigs of basil
2 sprigs of mint
1 tbsp. Umeboshi vinegar

### PREPARATION

Wash the endive, cut half into rounds and blend the other half. Peel
the avocado, remove the pit, cut into small pieces and put
in the blender. Add the rice milk, half the pepper and the Umeboshi
vinegar. Blend until smooth and then divide between the soup bowls.
Wash the spring onion and chili pepper.
Cut the beet into matchsticks, the remaining pepper into pieces,
the chili pepper into rounds, and the pineapple flesh and Belgian
endive into pieces. Decorate the soup with a sprinkling of spring onion
and a few aromatic herbs.
Wash and peel the cucumbers, cut into pieces and pass them through
the centrifugal juicer together with the remaining herbs; season
with freshly squeezed lemon juice and serve with the soup.
A triumph of flavors and vegetable garden aromas, this soup is a great
substitute for a very low-calorie first course!

Preparation time: 15' - Difficulty: easy

# FENNEL, ORANGE, CHICORY AND SPINACH SOUP

INGREDIENTS FOR **2** SERVINGS

1 head of chicory (about 200 g)
2 fennels
2 oranges
1/2 cup (100 g) spinach
salt and pepper

PREPARATION

Cut the oranges in half and squeeze half of them.
Put the juice in a bowl.
Wash the fennel and cut into pieces; put half to one side and pass
the other half through the centrifugal juicer.
Wash the chicory and spinach and, as for the other ingredients, pass
just half through the centrifugal juicer.
Mix all the juices together, salt and pepper to taste and stir.
Put the remaining pieces of orange, without the peel, and the fennel,
spinach and chicory into a bowl and serve.
An appetizing snack, rich in chlorophyll and vitamin C, retinol, folic
acid. This low-calorie soup is also extremely thirst-quenching
thanks to the high water content of the ingredients.

Preparation time: 15' - Difficulty: easy

# ZUCCHINI SOUP WITH LEMON, APPLE AND ORANGE

**INGREDIENTS FOR 2 SERVINGS**

1 apple
4 small zucchini
1 orange
1 lemon
1 tbsp. extra virgin olive oil
salt and pepper

**PREPARATION**

Wash and dry the apple and zucchini. Peel the apple,
remove the core and seeds, and cut into pieces.
Use a mandoline to slice the three zucchini in the form
of spaghetti and put in a bowl.
Cut the lemon and orange in half, cut two slices of orange and two
slices of lemon and put them to one side for decoration.
Squeeze the lemon and orange and pour the juice into the blender,
slice and add the remaining zucchini, the apple, oil,
salt and pepper to taste.
Blend until uniformly smooth, add to the zucchini spaghetti, mix
together and divide between the bowls. Decorate with the slices
of citrus fruit and serve.
A fantastic thirst-quenching and filling snack that is light and fresh.

Preparation time: 20' - Difficulty: easy

# ALPHABETIC INDEX
# OF RECIPES

# ALPHABETIC INDEX OF INGREDIENTS

All the photographs are by Cinzia Trenchi except

Timer image: Lucian Coman/123RF; page 5: Tetiana Vitsenko/123RF;
page 7: Serg_v/123RF; page 9: Anna Kucherova/123RF; page 121: Inga Nielsen/123RF;
page 123: Chris Elwell/123RF; page 128: Irina Ukrainets/123RF

# CINZIA
# TRENCHI

A naturopath, freelance journalist and photographer specializing in wine and food itineraries, Cinzia Trenchi has collaborated in the writing of numerous recipe books published by Italian and foreign publishing houses. A passionate cook, she has also worked for many Italian magazines covering regional, traditional, macrobiotic and natural cuisine specialties, providing both the text and the photographs, and including dishes of her own creation. Her recipe books include original and creative meals. They propose new flavor associations and unusual pairings that result in unique preparations that keep with the spirit of flavor without forgetting the nutritional properties of foods, in order to achieve the best equilibrium during a meal and the consequent improvement in well-being. She lives in Monferrato, in the Piedmont region, in a home immersed in greenery. Using the flowers, aromatic herbs and vegetables grown in her garden, she prepares original sauces and condiments, in addition to decorations for her dishes, allowing herself to be guided by the seasons and her knowledge of the earth's fruits. With White Star Publishers she has published "Gluten-Free, Gourmet Recipes"; "Fat-Free, Gourmet Recipes"; "Chili Pepper, Moments of Spicy Passion"; "My Favorite Recipes"; "Smoothies & Juices, Health and Energy in a Glass"; "Hamburgers, 50 Easy Recipes"; "Mug Cakes, Sweet & Savory Recipes"; "Detox, Practical Tips and Recipes for Clean Eating"; "Superfoods, Healthy, Nourishing and Energizing Recipes", "Vegan Cookbook, Tasty Recipes and Tips for Your Health" and "Yogurt, 50 Easy Recipes".

# NOTES

127

# WHITE STAR PUBLISHERS

WS White Star Publishers® is a registered trademark
property of White Star s.r.l.

© 2016 White Star s.r.l.
Piazzale Luigi Cadorna, 6 - 20123 Milan, Italy
www.whitestar.it

Translation and Editing: TperTradurre s.r.l.

ISBN 978-88-544-1017-6
1 2 3 4 5 6   20 19 18 17 16

Printed in China

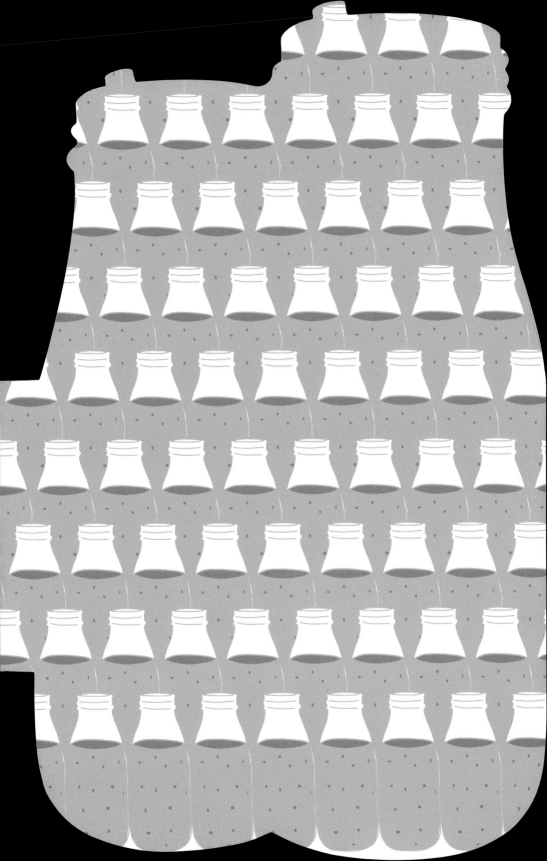

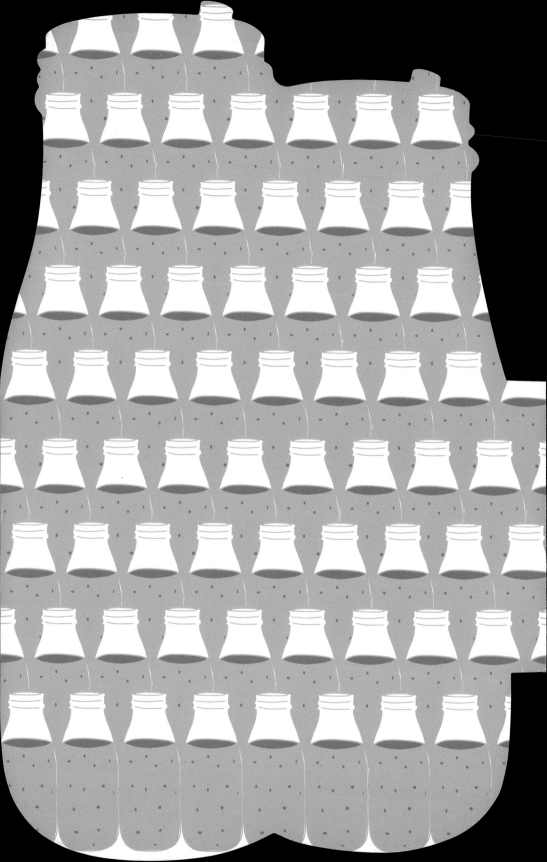